Tradition and Transformation

A Philosophical Treatise

Based on the Ifa Religious System

TRADITION AND TRANSFORMATION

A Philosophical Treatise
Based on the Ifa Religious System

Baba Koleoso Karade

KÂNDA MUKÛTU BOOKS

© Copyright 2001 by Baba Koleoso Karade.

Editorial Production: Roger/Rudolph Francis

Edited by: Oloye Baba Ifa Karade

Interior/Cover Design and Composition: Mulberry Tree Press, Inc.

Library of Congress Control Number: 2001 130342

Baba Koleoso Karade

Traditions and Transformation
A Philosophical Treatise Based on the Ifa Religious System

ISBN 1–890157–27–9

1. African (Yoruba) Religion, Spirituality
2. African Ancestors
2. Yoruba Tradition

Cover Photo: Mask of the Kono people of Guinea (west Africa), representing rebirth as a result of initiation.

Printed in Canada.

Father/Mother, God,
I turn now giving thanks to you for this gift of life.
I give thanks now for the sacrifices of my Ancestors.
Were it not for them, I would not be!

I thank those strong Africans for enduring the march
to the slave dungeons of West Africa.
I thank them for enduring the pain, confusion, darkness,
loneliness, and community separation they experienced
while waiting to pass through "The Door of No Return."

I thank them for enduring the journey through
the "Middle Passage."
I thank them for their strength, determination,
tenacity, and love.

I thank them for enduring the horrors of Slavery,
for giving birth to me in the cotton fields of Mississippi
and Arkansas, the peanut fields of Georgia,
the tobacco fields of Kentucky,
and the sugar cane fields of Louisiana.

I give thanks to all my Ancestors, both known and unknown.
May my life be a testimony to them and their vision for humanity.

This book is dedicated to my wonderful Grand Daughter,
Ameera. Thank you for your return, you have so much to teach me.

Peace & Love
Koleoso

ACKNOWLEDGEMENTS

Modupe to the Creator Olodumare, the prophet Orunmila, the Orisha, Ancestors and the enlightened Elders of this faith.

To my Mother for her strength and my Father for his confidence

To My Wife, Rashidah and my children, Jashed, Ayesha, and Yasmeen. Thank you for giving me the honor of being your Husband and father.

To Taalib El-Amin, Na'im Akbar, Don Offutt, Chester Grundy and Hendrix Floyd (brothers who have supported and encouraged my Ifa quest).

To the Ancestral Sprits of the Java House, your story will be told and you will be honored.

To the Ile Tawo Lona family, thank you for accepting me "Home."

To Ifasina Oduyemi Karade, Thank you for pointing me to the Healing Waters of Yemoja.

To **Oloye "Baba" Ifa Karade**. It is said that the lowest stone in the structure carries the most weight. It has been Baba Ifa Karade who has placed so many of us on his shoulders and carried us. It has been he who with courage and dedication accepted his call and paved the way for us. I thank Olodumare for Baba, who with love showed me that I had just enough knowledge to get to the Temple door. Who with wisdom opened a portal for me in July of 1998 and allowed me to walk through and submit to Shango. It is to Olodumare, Orisha, and Egun that I thank for placing me in the hands of such a wise and masterful teacher. It is with love and respect that I say to you Baba, Modupe!

TABLE OF CONTENTS

Ise Olorun tobi

God's work is great and mighty

TRADITION AND TRANSFORMATION

A Philosophical Treatise

Based on the Ifa Religious System

INTRODUCTION

When we speak of Rites of Passage and Initiations, we learn that separation is an important aspect. The young initiates are separated from their 'normal' surroundings so the new knowledge can be imparted to them without distractions. In some societies initiation into secret societies involves learning a new language and receiving a new name. What of the Cosmic Rite of Passage of a people? Over 450 years ago, we were separated from our normal surroundings for several generations. We have learned some difficult lessons!!

Addressing the issue of separation and Rites of Passage, John S. Mbiti writes in his book, *African Religions and Philosophy*,

> "The youth are ritually introduced to the art of communal living. This happens when they withdraw from other people to live alone in the forest or in specifically prepared huts away from the villages. They go through a period of withdrawal from society, absence from home, during which time they receive secret instruction before they are allowed to rejoin their relatives at home. This is a symbolic experience of the process of dying, living in the spirit world and being reborn (resurrected). The rebirth, that is the act of rejoining their families, emphasizes and dramatizes that the young people are now new; they have new personalities, they have lost their childhood, and in some societies they even receive completely new names." [1]

My quest is to show that while this process happens with youths in African societies, I see that it has happened to an entire race of people. In like manner, our forefathers were forcefully withdrawn from their people and brought to the western hemisphere to live in the forest or specifically pre-pared huts (slave shacks). Mbiti says, "during this separation initiates received secret instruction before they are allowed to rejoin their relatives at home." Have we Africans in America received secret instruction? Yes! We came out of the belly of the beast and we have learned how to survive culturally intact in the midst of this material opulence. Those who have been blessed to come through the generations of negative indoctrination know full well the dangers of this western mentality. You will find these spiritually mature and con-scious initiates on every level of American society. Mbiti makes the point that this withdrawal is a symbolic experi-ence of the process of dying, living in the spirit world and being reborn (resurrected). Our process of dying occurred when we were taken from our Motherland, totally stripped of all knowledge of self, culture and kind. Our living in the western hemisphere is symbolic to living in the spirit world. Our rebirth began when we began to reclaim our cultural heritage. Many of us are being resurrected and are now ready to return home not only mentally and spiritually, but also physically. It will be our family who accepts us back and who will show us our place in the world village.

I refer to this as a Cosmic Rite of Passage and Initiation be-cause it is by the will of the Divine Creative Principle that it happened! Why? Why would God, a merciful God, a loving God allow a people to experience what we have experienced if it were not for a higher purpose? Could it be that we have gone through a 450 year Rite of Passage and Iinitiation that we might become the prototype of the resurgence of the authentic human being; of humanity itself.

If the characteristics of all my Ancestors are carried in my DNA, then it is very conceivable that I am that same Ancestor who was enslaved! Enslaved for the Cosmic Rite of Passage! That I have endured generations of separation from my people and myself. That I have lived in this forest or spirit world.

I have often heard Dr. Na'im Akbar say during his lectures that, "we were not supposed to be here." We have survived the most horrible conditions that a people could endure! Could it be that the spirits had/have a plan for us? We would say so! History teaches us of the 100 million that physically died in the Middle Passage, the millions that died during slavery. However, today millions remain mentally and spiritually dead. Yet, there are those whom spirit has touched who have opened their eyes and have survived totally! These individuals are wide awake and ready to return home.

Speaking further about his initiation, Malidoma says,

> "I knew that my survival was dependent upon a supreme effort not to resist the initiation process or to set up rules and measurements to control the flow of information presented to me." [2]

Could it be that one of the things that keeps the majority of our people dead and unable to survive this cosmic initiation process are the rules and measurements that we have set up to control the flow of information presented to us? That if it does not agree with euro-religious dogma then the information is taboo? As a result, we never see the larger picture. We never see God's vision and purpose for us. We must not resist what the

Ancestors are bringing to us via our Cosmic Rites of Passage and initiation. As we learn of the great religions of home, as we learn of Yoruba, Akan, Kamit, etc., we must not seek to control the flow. We must open up and allow the Ancestors to show us the way.

The 450 year Rite of Passage and Initiation is over; it is time for the new initiates to return to the people. The information that follows is a minor attempt to allow the information to flow and not resist the initiation process any longer. May Olodumare, the Orishas and the Ancestors forever guide my way.

CHAPTER 1

Praise to the Elders

I. Iba se ori ire
*"Praise to the wise ones for the blessing
of their wisdom"*

On August 17, 1996, I wrote,

"I have long sought a way to make a contribution to the collective struggle of African people. I chose not to allow myself to get pigeonholed into my particular aspect of the political nature of this struggle. Recognizing that all aspects of the struggle are valid and necessary, I chose to remain neutral and open in my identification with any particular aspect of this struggle. Yet, I was very focused and directed in the need for manifestation and cultural reclamation. It is said, "if you do not know where you are going, any road will take you there." I knew that I was heading home to the realization of my lost cultural identity."

The journey towards the reclamation of one's cultural legacy is a most rewarding and welcoming experience. It is a journey that must be taken if one is to function in this world peacefully. A rebirth is experienced with each step toward cultural reclamation. The richness, the completeness, the satisfaction and rewards are so tremendous. It is as if our Ancestors are waiting with open arms and smiling faces as we, Africans born in America, discover the rich cultural treasures they left for us. Among these treasures is the Yoruba religion; a religion that our Ancestors brought to the western hemisphere and hid until the time was right. As Baba Ifa Karade points out in his book, *The Handbook of Yoruba Religious Concepts,*

> "It is important to note that the greatest percentage of Africans enslaved for New World labor came from the Yoruba nation. It is also important to note that a large percentage of those enslaved were war-political prisoners of elite classes of soldiers and warrior-priests. As a result, the New World became inundated with a people knowledgeable of their culture and who were initiated members of its higher teachings. It is of no small wonder that the Yoruba culture became the dominant theme of African-American transference." [3]

Our Ancestors hid and preserved this sacred treasure (Yoruba) in what is known as Santeria, Candomble, Voodoo and Lucumi. They hid it well until the time would come when their children, Africans born in America, would pick it up. The children would remove the protective wrappings of Catholicism and hold it up in all of its glory before the world. Those Africans born in America would bring this faith close to their breast and protect it vigorously, for it represents the bridge back home.

As a result of the study of Yoruba and high Egyptian religious systems, many African Americans now feel a calling to the priestly order, a calling that was successfully hidden in their consciousness. Dr. Na'im Akbar speaks of our genetic memory and how the telling of our story activates that genetic memory and we begin to function in accord with our true nature. Thus, cloaked into our genes are the ancient priests and priestesses of Ancient Egypt, Ifa, etc. The time will come when our griots and scholars would begin to tell our stories and awaken our Ancestral memory and we would return home to our faith, our religion, our God.

II. MODUPE EGUN
"I thank you Ancestors"

In a period of what seems to be a growing religiously flawed era perpetuated by individuals preying on the sincerity and weakness of others, there is a need for a sober reality check. We go to church each Sunday and we hear stories of heroes of faith. We learn of the faith of Daniel in the lion's den, we marvel at the faith of Abraham and we seek to pattern our lives behind the faith of Jesus. We pay homage to the Prophet Muhammad because he endured tremendous opposition in the establishment of Islam. We go to the Mosque and bear witness to the faith of Bilal as he bore witness to the oneness of Allah in the face of torture. Yet, we do not weep or bear witness to the strength of faith held by those African Ancestors that endured the horrors of the slave castles, the middle passage, and slavery.

Today, as we step into the political arena under the guise of religion, as we seek to become millionaires and psychological slave holders in the name of God, little or nothing is said regarding the tremendous faith and superior belief systems of our Ancestors. A faith and belief system which allowed them to endure the worst of horrors known to any people. Each Black History Month we go on superficial adolescent ego trips as we reach back in time to bring the accomplishments of our

Ancestors to the forefront. Yet, again little is said of the faith and belief systems of our Ancestors prior to the Arab and European invasions of Africa. We never stop to think, if our Ancestors gave the sciences to the world, if they gave the first written language, math, pyramids etc. to the world, then surely these great people had a belief system and gave that also.

We act as if we did not know God until we became Muslims and Christians. We continue to present the history and legacy of our people through Arab/Eurocentric eyes. How can we continue to convene great Africentric conferences, bring in world renowned Africentric scholars and yet have buses ready to shuttle conference goers to worship that which does not reflect us? How can we, in light of historical facts continue to clothe a European belief system in the cultural clothes of our Ancestors? Today, many who are culturally conscious walk around conferences with an apologetic attitude, as if we are sorry for being Yoruba, Akan, or Kamatic in our religious orientation. Again I ask you, what was the faith and belief system of those Africans who endured all the horrors of slavery? These individuals were not only able to survive misfortune, but they turned this misfortune into an advantage in their spiritual development.

Walter Houston Clark in his book, *The Psychology of Religion* points out;

> "But faith is not only a discrete and specific psychological function, but also to some degree a kind of conversation between the beliefs of the mind and acts of the organism, a resultant of tension between belief and action." [4]

Thus, it is easy to say that we believe in God, yet faith requires action on that belief. Our Ancestors knew that their be-

lief systems would assist them in surviving the horrors of slavery. In fact, their systems were based on thousands of years of
knowing. The faith of our Ancestors is something that we
should give serious consideration to. For a people to survive
the horrors of being captured, tortured, and enslaved speaks of
tremendous inner and external strength; a strength born of a
knowing faith.

Today, it seems that, for the most part, our faith is limited to
calling on God to assist us in our efforts to assimilate into this
material consciousness society. It seems that we are quick to
give thanks to God in public for our material blessings, partic-
ularly when these material goods place us on par with our
white counterparts. Does the fact that I drive a new car, live in
an upscale community and attend all the elitist social gather-
ings mean that God has blessed me because of my faith? Or
could it mean that my faith has been directed towards the ac-
quisition of these things? It seems that our Ancestors called on
their God just to make it through another day! To have the
courage to face another day of enslavement; to face another
day without their family, their home land, their culture, religion, and names. I contend that it was their intimate personal
knowing of their God and religion that gave rise to a faith that
helped them to endure. In the book, *Cutting Through Spiritual
Materialism*, Chogyam Trungpa says of faith:

> ". . . it could be definite confidence which cannot be
> destroyed. In the case of faith as confidence, there is a
> living reason to be confident. You do not expect that
> there will be a prefabricated solution mysteriously pre-
> sented to you. You work with existing situations with-
> out fear, without any doubt about involving yourself.
> This approach is extremely creative and positive. If you

have definite confidence, you are so sure of yourself that you do not have to check yourself. It is absolute confidence, real understanding of what is going on now, therefore you do not hesitate to follow other paths or deal in whatever way is necessary with each new situation." [5]

Could it be that our Ancestors had such faith? They were so confident that they were able to work with the existing situation of enslavement and captivity without fear. Now, this is not to say there was no fear, it is only to say that the fear was such that it did not incapacitate them, for had it incapacitated them then we would not be here today! They had a faith of confidence, a confidence born of thousand of years of knowing that their God would see them through. They had a real understanding of what was taking place and did not hesitate to follow other paths or deal in whatever ways that were necessary in the new situation. Also, it was their faith which allowed them to make the necessary adjustments that enabled them to survive the Middle Passage and slavery even unto this day ! The question becomes, what were the belief systems that gave rise to a faith of such confidence; and why have we not heard about it? In, *Imoye: A Definition Of The Ifa Tradition*, Baba Ifa Karade writes:

"Many Black scholars and religious leaders of the past and present are seemingly reluctant to speak of Before Christian era West Africa. As a result, the Black Movement did not have a great degree of West African ingredient to it and for the most part it still does not. The major components of liberation extracted from Judeo-Christianity, Islam, and East African realms have overshadowed the West African reality as a source of being and belonging for the post enslavement New World descendants. Again, very few scholars/leaders stepped out of their religious backgrounds and educational conditioning to express the philosophies, religions, and sciences of West Africa that originated hundreds of thousands of years BC. In fact, many set major obstacles to traditional African acceptance and development thereof." [6]

Thus, one reason we do not know of the faith and religious systems of our ancestors is because our scholars and religious leaders did not teach us of such. One can only wonder why? Could it be as Amos Wilson says in his book, *"The Falsification of Afrikan Consciousness,*

"Religions become the opiates of the oppressed and conversely, opiates become their religions, and addictions to both materially benefit their oppressors and exploiters. The fantasy, nursed in the overheated imagination of oppressed Afrikans and often hypocritically encouraged by their oppressors, that they and their oppressors will one day live blissfully as one, is the most pernicious hoax of all. For it motivates many Afrikans to blithely nurture and protect the system which exploits them and blinds them to its intrinsically evil purpose and ultimately deadly intent." [7]

Could it be that the failure of scholars and leaders to speak of West African religions is a manifestation of their subconscious acceptance of this pernicious hoax.

Marimba Ani says in her book *YURUGU,*

"Christianity was a more refined tool for the selling

of European imperialism. There are certain traits that have made for the success of European civilization in its quest for supreme dominance and control of others. It is a culture based on an ideology of superficial change. This allows its hegemony to expand while being maintained." [8]

For the most part, it is our failure to learn of the belief systems of our Ancestors that helps to spread European nationalism. On the surface, this European culture is saying that we are all equal in the eyes of God while at the same time seeking and maintaining psychological dominance over us. We have been made to think of the religions of West Africa as backward and superstitious. Of this Baba Ifa Karade states,

"The African religion was and continues to be projected as dark, magical, sensational, and for all intent and purpose un–Godly hence, true deliverance and salvation can only be gained from the Christian religion and acceptance into and by the western mind-set." [9]

As a result, we run from our traditional religions when in reality these were the religions that we brought to this country with us. These were the religions that gave rise to the faith that assisted us in surviving the horrors of the enslavement period. In an address to The 5Th World Congress Of Orisha Tradition and Culture, Baba Ifa Karade states,

"The 400 year enslavement of the Yoruba nation by the Europeans brought to the New World the vestiges of Ifa and the Orisha Tradition. Ifa and Orisha survived in spite of the brutal physical and psychological damage caused by the enslavers. The potency of thousands of years of faith and devotion to the Orisha as deities along with the tenacious holding on to Africa as the center for cultural relativity and self-awareness led to the ultimate victory over the slave system's strategy of genocide."

Thus, it was our faith and devotion to Ifa and the Orisha tradition which helped us survive slavery. However, because of our desire to succeed in this European culture we began to unknowingly assist European imperialism. We continued to merge with its racial value system under the cover of religion. We turned our backs on our cultural heritage because it did not fit within the European worldview. All we need do is study history and see what has been the outcome of those who gave up their traditions and culture in an effort to fit into the European interpretation of reality. They are still subjects of a system that exploits and dominates them. It is dangerous for us to live in denial as if our people did not have belief systems prior to Christianity and Islam.

"There are those of us who are made ashamed of our history of enslavement, who are made ashamed by the distorted presentation of Afrikan history (which is why the European distorts it and presents it the way he does), are made to think that prior to slavery we were essentially culturally invisible and savage and only achieved visibility and civility when the European came on the scene. Many of us attempt to repress any knowledge of our American slave experience. But we should heed the fact that a person and people who suffer from social amnesia live lives that are determined by fear, anxiety, terror and trauma. When we attempt to escape our history because we are afraid of it, when we escape knowledge because it terrifies and makes us feel ashamed, then it is terror and fear and shame that determine our lives. We live, not in terms of our reality and in terms of the integration of our reality but in terms of what we are afraid of, i.e., what we are ashamed of, what we are trying to hide, what we are trying not to confront ourselves with. Life is then lived in terms of denial, in terms of escape and addiction." [10]

The more we run from our history, the more we involve ourselves in self destructive behavior. We were made to believe that we were savages, that our life styles were uncivilized and that we needed to be civilized in the light of our oppressor. We developed a conscious denial of our past greatness and accepted our oppressor's interpretation of who we were. This acceptance of our so-called inferiority gave rise to a tremendous self-hate that still haunts us today. This self- hate is manifested in the destruction we see in our communities, the murders, deaths, escapism into European cultural expressions of relationships, fashion, and social behavior.

The study of our history will reveal that among our Ancestors who were forced to come to this country, there were those who refused to give up their cultural heritage. They escaped the plantations and made their way to the hills. They became the freedom fighters who established the Maroon societies. There in the hills, they preserved much of our cultural traditions.

"They did not endeavor to define themselves in western terms; terms which emphasized the necessity of Euro-centric religious icons and worship, western cultural practices, western rites of passage, education, and overall live-style. As a result, the African cultural motifs were preserved by that minority of "maroon" and wisened elders who maintained the Ifa and Orisha traditions; traditions which were slowly disappearing through absorption and alterations to fit Euro-centric understandings, laws, and entertainment." [11]

Our culture has been preserved and maintained to some degree, yet we still refuse to embrace it. If Ifa and Orisha worship got our Ancestors through the horrors of the enslavement period surely it will get us through this period of psychological slavery.

"The Ifa religion provided healing and foundation during enslavement. It served as a constant reminder of who we are and just how important it is for us to relate to the forces of life and identify with it through our own likeness. During the time when we were being stripped of our self worth, it was our tradition that prevented us from committing total self-annihilation. The worship of Orisha healed our spiritual constitution and gave us some semblance of the reality that it is important for the deities of a people to look like and reflect the self-image of those people. The wisdom of Ifa, as expressed through the Sacred Odu, challenged us to remain true to our moral and righteous construct even in the face of immorality and degradation. In essence, the religious and philosophical basis for our African existence revolved, and continues to revolve around the tenets and fundamental concepts of the Yoruba religious practice. Ifa was the major ingredient in the healing process of the enslaved African; and now it must be made available for the disillusioned African as well." [12]

—Baba Ifa Karade

"5th Orisha World Congress," San Fransico Ca., 1997

It will be our returning to our cultural traditions that will heal us, our families and communities. Yet, this return must be lead by individuals who have the same courage and determination as those Ancestors who fled the plantations and formed the free societies in the hills. These individuals must have the will to escape the plantation of European cultural interpretations of reality and return to our ways and traditions. Their thinking must reflect the same desire for freedom and independence as was demonstrated by those who formed the Maroon communities. They must be willing to lead the way, however it is imperative that they must first be healed. They must be healed of the deep psychological wounds that keep even them from totally embracing the traditions of our Ancestors. It is one thing to embrace a tradition because it is a fad and made popular by the dominant society for the purposes of further exploitation. It is yet another thing to accept a tradition as a life style, as a means of healing and bringing one in closer contact with their purpose for being.

> "The major emphasis of Ifa has always been that of bringing the self back into harmony with the saving grace of the divine forces of creation."

To be brought back into harmony with the saving grace of the divine forces of creation suggests that one has been taken out of harmony. The lack of knowledge about our history, is responsible, in part, for this tragedy. The reclaiming of our cultural traditions will provide the medicine which will help us to heal our souls.

CHAPTER 2

THE SPIRITUAL PATH

I. THE SPIRITUAL CALLING

Shamanism has been referred to as the most ancient of mankind's religious, medical, and psychological disciplines. The term used to refer to specific groups of healers in diverse cultures, who are sometimes called medicine men, witch doctors, sorcerers, wizards, magicians, or seers, is shaman. According to Roger N. Walsh:

> "Shamanism can be defined as a family of traditions whose practitioners focus on voluntarily entering altered states of consciousness in which they experience themselves or their spirit(s), traveling to other realms at will and interacting with other entities in order to serve their community." [13]

It is the shaman who travels between realms to visit spirits, to capture lost souls, sit with Ancestors, and to bring back knowledge that will benefit his/her community. In Kenya, the healers or shamans live in the communities that believe in them. Everything they do is communal and interactive. The same can be said of all shamans. However, while shamanism is slowly gaining acceptance, it is not a part of modern western culture. As such, our communities are left with little to actually and tangibly believe.

While spiritual seers have always been part of the fabric of the African–American community, they were not always accepted. As such, they had to function on the perimeters of euro-centric society. They were viewed as strange, weird, or crazy, never holding the central communal position of honor and respect that their indigenous counterparts held. However, the spirits and the Ancestors continue to call African-Americans to the path of shamanism.

The Ausar/Auset Society, founded in 1970 by Ra Un Nefer Amen, is a spiritual society which believes, and in fact trains its members in spirit and ancestral communication. A principle function of the priest and priestess within the Ausar/Auset Society is to access the Spirits, Deities and Ancestors in order to provide guidance for the community. Ra Un Nefer Amen reminds us that a prime requirement for leadership within the traditional African community was the ability of the leader to house a deity or spirit. He states in *Metu Neter Vol. 1*:

> The Man (and all others - living and deceased) who will lead the people must be initiated into the ability to serve as a vehicle through which the Supreme Being and its agencies (the Deities) will govern the People. All leaders must, therefore, be masters of divine law, and priests of the shrines of deities. [14]

To adhere to this was/is a semblence of insurance that the Supreme Being was guiding the community and not the ego or personality of the leader. Think how great this would be today if our leaders were spiritually evolved enough to allow the spirits and deities to guide the nation instead of their immature egos. However, that is an entirely different subject. Ra Un Nefer Amen further states that all African societies and communities had the knowledge of how to communicate with the deceased. In fact, this communication with the deceased and spirit world occupied a central role in the life of all African and indigenous people. Again, to demonstrate the importance of this ability to communicate with the spirit world and how it is so much a part of our cultural heritage, Ra Un Nefer Amen says,

> "At prescribed times, rituals are preformed by the African kings (Heru) and their royal priesthood to communicate with the spirits of the deceased kings (the Ausars) in order to receive their advice. This type of ritual is incorrectly called, by Western scholars, 'ancestor worship.' It must be called *ancestor communication rituals*." [15]

Thus, we see that spirit and ancestral communication is part of our cultural heritage. However, unlike the shaman, who receives honor and respect, today our seers and mediums do not occupy the central role in our lives and communities, as they should. With the continued work of the Ausar/Auset Society, Yoruba communities, and Afri-religious centers this will change.

The "call" to shamanism varies from culture to culture. However, it generally includes dreams, visions, heredity, unusual physical appearances, and illness, such as epilepsy, and unexpected recovery from severe illness. The central theme involved with the "call" to shamanism is the future shaman dies, is dismembered, cleansed, put back together, and reborn. It is said that one has to "die" and be reborn to become a shaman.

Much too often, the "call" can be ignored. Of this Walsh writes,

"The call to shamanism may be received with con-
siderable ambivalence, and those who receive it may
be regarded as 'doomed to inspiration.' Many of the
elect attempt to decline the invitation at first. This is
what Joseph Campbell termed 'refusal of the call.'
However, the spirits, symptoms, or dreams may be
distressingly persistent and eventually win out. Indeed, many shamanic traditions, like many hero traditions, hold that refusal of the call can result in sick-
ness, insanity, or death. One of the earliest shamanic
researchers, Bogoras, claimed that "the rejection of
the "spirits"" is much more dangerous even than the
acceptance of their call." [16]

Therefore, it is the "spirits" that chose the shaman. While
many individuals have chosen shamanism for themselves, usu-
ally because of the power and position in the community that
the shaman holds, it is said they are less potent masters than
those shamans who are chosen by the spirits. While there are
aspects of the "call" that can be ignored, the shamanic initiation crisis cannot. This initiation crisis explodes in the life of
the would be shaman with life shattering force. It disintegrates
the old equilibrium and identity and demands birth of the
new. This initiation crisis is characterized by a number of psychological experiences which include heightened sensitivity
and perception. The would be shaman can begin to exhibit unusual, even bizarre, dangerous, and life-threatening behavior.
All of this could lead to weeks, months, or even years of un-
predictable chaos that disrupts his/her life, the life of their family, and the community to which they belong. The "call" may
be abrupt or gradual. Of this Mircea Eliade writes:

"There are sicknesses, attacks, dreams, and hallucinations that determine a shaman's career in a very short time. On the other hand, sometimes there is not exactly an illness but rather a progressive change in behavior. The candidate becomes meditative, seeks solitude, sleeps a great deal, seems absent-minded, has prophetic dreams and sometimes seizures. All these symptoms are only the prelude to the new life that awaits the unwitting candidate. His behavior, we may add, suggests the first signs of a mystical vocation, which are the same in all religions and too well known to dwell upon." [17]

While the western culture regards this type of behavior as evidence of severe psychopathology, in shamanic cultures this crisis is interpreted as proof that the victim is destined to be a shaman. It is argued by many western observers of shamanism that the shaman is a madman. However, the converse of this is that the shaman is one who was sick and has cured him/herself and is much better off than he/she was before. In curing themselves, they are now ready to cure others. With the help of spirit guides and ancestors, the shaman travels through different realms of reality, learning different ways of healing, among a host of other things.

In recent years, many African-American psychologists, such as Na'im Akbar, Wade Nobles, Bobby Wright, Amos Wilson and others have worked and are working to change western standards and interpretations of shamism. Yet, much work needs to be done before we can accept fully a brother or sister who talks, walks, and communicates with and in the spirit realm. To illustrate this point further, D. Patrick Miller writes of an experience he had with the African Shaman, Malidoma Patrice Some and his wife Sobonfu:

"I happen to use the word "schizophrenic" and Sobonfu, who began learning English upon her arrival in America only three years ago, asks me what it means. It means someone who is psychiatrically diagnosed as having a split mind. They hear voices in their head and tend to be withdrawn from daily life. It's very difficult for them to function in society. "In your culture," Sobonfu quietly observes. In her culture, people who often hear disembodied voices are naturally assumed to be talking with the spirit world and receive special attention and respect to help translate to valuable messages they are tuning in." [18]

It now becomes clear that there is a need for us to examine how we treat those among us whom we classify as crazy. Think of those members of your family. Look into your family history and you may have someone who talked with spirits and people said they were crazy. I know, in my family, there is told the story of my great-grandmother, who was full blooded Cherokee, who used to talk to herself, but when you came up to her, she could read you like a book. However, the family said she was crazy and did not pay attention to her. Think of all the valuable spiritual knowledge we are losing because we are following the standard that is set by someone else. Now, I do realize that there is the possibility that many of us do need some psychological help, however, that help has to come from those who are familiar with the way of our ancestors and the "call" of the spirits.

So many of us are being "called" by the Ancestors, however, we do not know what is taking place. Let me give you a final example. In an interview with "Body, Mind, Spirit

Magazine", January 1995, Malidoma Some was asked the question:

"Are you saying that we have generations of Ancestors who have died and are trapped in the middle world, or in an area of the cosmos where they cannot progress? And are they still calling on us for help? We, of course, don't know this, and so our energy is being sapped . . ."

His reply was:

"Challenged in all kinds of different subtle ways. But all of these ups and downs are the direct results of the dead's attempt at sending the message that you need to shed tears for them. . . ." [19]

As I review my individual life, I see tremendous ups and downs and perhaps you do also. I see times of trying to reach the goal and never making it, constant disappointments and constantly trying, but never getting anywhere. My Ancestors are calling and I have listened. I need to shed tears for them, I need to pour water for them, I need to help them on their way!! Caitlin Matthews writes in, *Singing the Soul Back Home, Shamanism in Daily Life.*

"Many of our present problems derive from inherited ancestral patterns. So we need to stand in right relationship to our forebears, give them their due and pay them respect." [20]

What are the inherited ancestral patterns that we carry and are called to change? Think of the unfinished business that our Ancestors have taken to the other side with them. Think of the pain and confusion that has been caused due to ignorance, greed, or malicious intent. What of the unfinished business the ancestors have with us and we with them? I recall hearing Sister Marimba Ani, of Hunter College, say that we need to do rituals for the young brothers and sisters who are dying at a young age from crime. Think of them being ushered into another reality not ready and not knowing where they are. Think of the fear and confusion. Yes, they too are calling us to pour water for them. While you may not be called to the life of the shaman, you are being called to honor God, Orishas and your Ancestors. They will keep knocking at your door until you answer. I pray that you will have the insight and courage to do so.

II. Touched by the Holy

As we have seen, it is the shamanic initiation crisis that explodes into the life of the would be shaman with life shattering force. This crisis destroys the old equilibrium and idenity and demands that the individual be born again. It is our thesis that the Near-Death-Experience is a shamanic initiation crisis in which the individual is called and initiated into the early stages of shamanism. Dr. Kenneth Ring in his book, *Heading Towards Omega*, states,

> The spiritual core of the NDE is so awesome and overwhelming that the person who experiences it is at once and forever thrust into an entirely new mode of being. . . . After that experience, the person can never again return to the former way of being— though some would like to. No longer can a person

take refuge in the comfort of the conventional views and values of society.

The individual who has experienced a Near-Death-Experience understands that beliefs are irrelevant, because beliefs are mere ideas that are substituted for knowledge. Like the shaman, the NDEr knows there are other realities. While many try to conform to the world that they left, they, in time, know that they must answer to the Call of the Drum that they hear, even though the drum is different than all of those around them.

In many cases, we have been so blinded by our (Western) cultural assumptions that individuals who have had a Near-Death-Experience in the African-American community find themselves in a no man's land. There is no support for them. They are labeled as psychotic and left to wander aimlessly in this Western world looking for someone who understands. Often, through faith in God and the Ancestors alone, they continue to move through each day. They know their perception of reality is different and that they must live what they know, even if it means living and walking alone. A shaman is a lone wolf. Individuals who have Near-Death Experiences are people who know and they become what they know, their knowledge lives and grows within them. The NDE causes a total transformation in the life of the individual. During the Near-Death Experience, the individual is transported to another reality.

"Students of shamanism—the ancient and virtual universal cultural tradition whose initiations and techniques are said to provide access to a nonsensory world beyond death—claim to know. They find the basic elements of the NDE to be inherent in the shaman's journey and in principle available to anyone who finds himself in the kind of altered state that shamanic practice seeks to induce." [21]

Also, the German writer on shamanism, Holger Kalweit says:

"In the near death state, the out-of-body experience, and during the journey to the Beyond [that is, in shamanic journeys], we are confronted by real phenomena of consciousness and not just by symbols of the unconscious." [22]

Many, who have had Near-Death-Experiences and journeyed to the Beyond, report seeing relatives, Angels, Spirits and central to all of this is the experience with the "White Light". Among other things, the light has been described as loving, warm, wonderful, peaceful, providing security, etc. Please understand that this is an experience that cannot be adequately described. In the words of Kenneth Ring:

"The NDE is then, not merely an experience that becomes a cherished memory that people may later take comfort in. It is not even just an experience that "changes one's life." It is one's life. And it becomes the source of one's true being in the world." [23]

The light has become my life. The quest for spiritual realization is the essence of who I have become as a result of two Near-Death Experiences. I, like so many others, am trying to answer the "call" and let the light shine in and through me. It is the NDE that allows one to see his/her immortality. It allows you to become conscious of being conscious. It takes you to the edge of the universe and allows you to look out into infinity and realize that you and it are one and the same. It is the Near-Death Experience that causes a total transformation in the life of the individual.

In comparing this to what happens to the shaman when he/she journeys to the Beyond Holger Kalweit writes:

> "The Shaman's near-death experience is also a transformation. He returns from the Beyond with wise counsel, revelations, and messages from the dead. For many shamans, the ascent to heaven or the descent to the underworld are central initiatory experiences. They emerge from them as changed persons upon whom the beings of the Beyond have bestowed special powers." [24]

Thus, like the shaman, individuals come back from their journey to the Beyond with tools for their new vocation. All, or most, realize they are "called" to a higher purpose in life, that they are called to serve all of humanity. As a result, the Near-Death Experience can be viewed as a form of initiation into shamanism. In his book *The Omega Project*, Dr. Ring writes:

> "The Shaman who Carol Zalekis aptly characterizes as 'the prototypical otherworld traveler,' is thus an individual who has learned consciously and voluntarily to enter into the same realm that the NDE is thrust into, without warning or preparation, by virtue of falling victim to a life-threatening crisis. Or to put it the other way around, the NDEr has been inadvertently initiated into the first stages of the Shaman's journey." [25]

Traditional shamanism maintains that an individual is primarily called to the vocation of a shaman by the spirits. It is the spirits that work with, guide, and initiate the would-be shaman. This is not to say would be shamans do not come under the guidance of practicing shamans—in fact, this is true in most indigenous cultures. They come under the guidance of a living Master while at the same time following and gaining power from their Spirit Guides. Yet, today in our society, it appears that shamanic initiation is taking place more in the spiritual realm, since there are few, if any, shamanic masters to learn from. If this is the case in the majority community, then the situation is much more acute in the African-American community. As a result, finding acceptance in one's community is both a major challenge and an initiatory test, for there is no one (master) to authorize you. It seems in today's society "authorization" or "validation" is the key. We like to know the qualifications of the individuals that come to us—what schools did they graduate from, how many degrees do they have? In essence, what worldly status do they hold? However, when we encounter the attitudes of indigenous people our viewpoints are turned upside-down. Among traditional shamans and shamanic societies, money and worldly education is irrelevant to status. The oral teachings are valued above the written word; and the messages from the Spirit realm are received, respected, and revered. In her book, *Singing the Soul Back Home*, Caitlin Matthews says,

> "Western civilization is a very complex environment to live within if we have Shamanic vocation. If we have a Shamanic vocation, our ordeals will definitely include the radical changing of our lifestyle and the effects that this will have upon our friends and family; it may involve putting up with ridicule and alienation." [26]

The call to shamanism via the Near-Death-Experience produces a dramatic change in lifestyle. The ridicule and alienation that one faces from family and friends can be such that it drives one to the brink. As was stated earlier, a lot of work has to be done before we can truly accept a brother or sister who works, talks, and communicates in the spiritual realm. It is so easy for us to hold up a standard of behavior that has been given to us by this Western world and seek to judge others with it. We, in the African American community, are notorious for looking into the lives of others and telling them how they should live. Yet, so few are ready for one who has been to the other side of this reality and has come back with vision and direction. These individuals are dismissed as crazy, weird, or out there!! This form of ridicule and nonacceptance by the community is one of the tests that the modern day shaman must endure. Sometimes, the greatest form of ridicule and alienation can come from the one you love the most, your mate. Yet, the individual who has been called and initiated into the path of the shaman via the Near-Death-Experience must find the courage to walk where the Spirit is leading them and have the faith to live what they see.

With our reclamation of our African and Native American spirituality and spiritual systems, an initiation as a result of the Near-Death-Experience may not be considered a valid initiation by many; however it is still an initiation. It is not our desire to get caught in the classification of initiations which would only serve to further divide us—i.e., "I was initiated by so-and-so." "I was initiated into this or that." "I was initiated at the Sun Dance." Our desire is only to say that the Near-Death-Experience is yet another form of initiation that should be taken into account. This is not to say that other initiations are not necessary in the life of the Near-Death Experiencer. You never know where the Spirit will lead you! This is only to say, there are many roads that lead to a city—let's not debate on the road that you took in getting to the city; let's rejoice over the fact that we are in the city together!

CHAPTER 3

THE PRIESTLY TRADITION

I. THE NATIVE SHAMAN AND THE ORISHA PRIEST

Africans born in America, for the most part, have degrees of Native American blood. As a result, we walk in two worlds. Running deep in our genes are those strong African Priests and Priestesses who survived the Middle Passage and slavery. Also, part of our genetic make up is that of the great Native American people with whom our enslaved African Ancestors formed bonds and found a new community in a strange land. Today, there is a need to synthesize these traditions and stand in the world as beacons of light calling the people back to tradition. The vanguards of this synthesizing process are the priest and priestesses of both traditions. These spiritual practitioners have the ability to transcend the religious dogmas that keep mankind from realizing it's true potential. While there are many spiritual practitioners, this discussion will be limited to that of the native Shaman and the Orisha Priest.

Essentially, the native Shaman and the Orisha priest are one and the same. Their cultural manifestations may differ, yet their roles and work in their communities are the same. Scholars have tended to distinguish between two polarities of religious specialization in reference to the priest and shaman. However, for Africans born in America of Native American blood, it is the overlapping and integration that is of paramount importance.

> ". . . a plains Indian Shaman is a ritual practitioner whose status is acquired through a personal communication from a supernatural being, whereas a priest does not necessarily have a face-to-face relationship with the spirit world but have competence in conducting rituals." [27]

Lessa and Vogt ([1950] 1965, p.410) expands on these differences,

> " A shaman's powers come by 'divine stroke,' a priest's power is inherited or is derived from the body of codified and standardized ritual knowledge that he learns from older priest and later transmits to successors." [28]

By applying the so-called differences to the lives of Africans born in America of Native American blood one can clearly see how the priest and shaman can be the same person. The majority of African-Americans come to our traditional ways via a "calling." Most if not all who have received a calling have had personal communication from a supernatural being, deceased ancestor, or guardian spirit. Like wise, most come from that body of codified and standardized ritual knowledge known as Christianity or Islam. As a result of this, the role of shaman/priest fits well.

C. Von Furer-Haimendorf writes,

> "The term 'Shaman,' now widely current in anthropo-

logical literature, was first applied to the religious practitioners of central and northern Asia, where the magico-religious life of most of the indigenous population traditionally centers on the Shaman. He is the dominating figure, though in many tribes there are also priests concerned with the performance of animal sacrifices, and every head of a family is also the head of the domestic cult. The ecstatic state is considered to be the supreme religious experience, and the Shaman is the great master of ecstasy. Unlike persons possessed by spirits and temporarily in their power, the Shaman controls spirits. He is able to communicate with the dead, or with demons and nature spirits, without becoming their instrument." [29]

Thus, we see it is the Shaman that communicates with the dead and controls spirits. Now, central to Yoruba worship is the securing the favor of the Orishas (angelic forces). J. Olumibe Lucas writes in his book, *The Religion of the Yorubas,*

"The chief object of Yoruba religious worship is to secure the active favor of the gods, thereby ensuring the physical, mental, and spiritual welfare of the worshipper. The belief is strong that if worship is duly given to the gods and spirits, they in turn will fulfill their own part of the 'commerce' by granting the worshipper his heart's desire." [30]

The question becomes who in the Yoruba tradition can a believer turn to for the securing of the Orisha's favor ? It is the priestly and the babalawos who have the responsibility of interacting with the Orishas, Spirits and Ancestors on behalf of the believers.

While the Native Shaman and the Yoruba Priest both enjoy respect and honor from their respective communities, this honor and respect does not come easy. The Shaman, like the Priest, must go through an extensive period of training and education. It may take a certain number of years to reach a level of proficiency in Shamanic or Priestly responsibilities; yet it is a lifetime of learning and seeking harmony with the divine.

Africans born in America of Native American blood come from both cultures, as such we have the responsibility to learn both ways and give these cultural traditions back to our people in a manner that will liberate them from psychological oppression. In many respects, it is the lack of cultural guides that keep us from realizing our true potential. Today, there is a need for traditional seers and sages to rise up and shine as lights in the darkness; the people are looking but the lights are few. Those who have been called to the path of the shaman and of the priest have the responsibility of showing the people the way. They must realize that cultural education is vital to the success of any shaman, priest, priestess or babalawo. Lucas points out,

> "One of the reasons why the primitive Yoruba religion has resisted to some extent the onslaught of western civilization is the fact that it is maintained by organized and in some cases, a trained priesthood. The stronger and more intelligent the priesthood is, the more conservative the religion becomes." [31]

If Africans born in America of Native American blood are to liberate themselves from the shackles of cultural oppression brought on by western civilization, it will be via a trained priesthood. Priests and priestesses who stand in the world and draw from both traditions (Native American and African) bringing light unto the darkness.

II. The Journey

As was stated earlier, that many Africans born in America are feeling the call to the Priesthood. Many are returning and re-discovering their ancestral legacy. Central to this discovery is the complete survey of their ancestral lineage. Many will dis-cover that there is someone in that line who carried the spir-itual mantel of the family. Much to their surprise, they dis-cover that they are now being called to assume the mantel at this time in history. Malidoma Some writes,

> "Those who are knowledgeable will see in almost every family at least one person who functions as the receptacle of the energies from the Other World, one family member who has the sensitivity to be aware of, and respond to, the deeper spiritual and some-times physical needs of the family across generations. Sometimes these people are recognized as caretakers of the family. They are called on for every need any family member has, and, in some cases, blamed for problems that the family encounters. The life of these people is not easy. Often they see things that are very disturbing, including visions of departed loved ones. In the worst scenarios, they are deeply disturbed and worried about serious wrongs throughout the cul-ture. They feel danger all around them. In the in-digenous world, these people are the shamans, the shrine keepers, and the healers of the family tree. They are being hailed by family members and friends

in this world, and by departed ancestors from the Other World who need healing." [31]

The majority of those among the priestly of Ifa, Orisha, or any indigenous spiritual discipline fall within this example. They are being called back to the traditional ways of our ancestors, they are being called to be the healers of their families, community and humanity. All throughout history it has been our Prophets, Messengers, Ministers, Sages, Medicine People, Healers, and Shamans that have called humanity to God's way. Today, more than ever, we need to heed the call of our ancestors and become healers; healers of ourselves, our families, communities, and humanity. It is as Ayi Kwei Armah writes,

" A healer needs to see beyond the present and tomorrow. He needs to see years and decades ahead. Because healers work for results so firm they may not be wholly visible till centuries have flowed into millennia. Those willing to do this necessary work, they are the healers of our people." [32]

Those who are called and accept may not see the results immediately, yet they will experience a "coming home" feeling in their soul. Of this call Baba Karade says in, *The Handbook of Yoruba Concepts,*

" There are different reasons why one is called to the priesthood. Some are called for spiritual reasons that involve only themselves and they work very little with others; some are called to be as messengers (Ojise Olorun); others are called to serve the Orisha in order to save themselves or loved ones from grave illnesses." [33]

III. THE YORUBA ILEKES

As Baba Ifa Karade has told me in personal instruction, " our Ancestors are always calling us to service, are we sensitive enough to answer?" Besides serious study, according to Baba Ifa, receiving the Ilekes (religious beads) is the first step of an actual commitment made by the novice towards the priesthood. Ifa/Yoruba and all of its derivatives (Santeria, Vodun, Candomble, and Lucumi) involve a progressive system of initiations. This system provides the novice with the protection of the Orishas (Angelic emanations of the Creator manifesting through nature) and an increasing knowledge of the various practices and beliefs of the religion. Baba Ifa points out,

> "Five Ilekes are presented ceremoniously to the initiate. Each Ileke represents an Orisha: white-Obatala; black and red-Elegba; yellow-Oshun; blue-Yemoja; red and white-Shango. The Ilekes are consecrated by the presiding priest/priestess. Ewe (herbs), ebo (sacrificial blood), and efun (sacred earth) are made into a solution (omiero). The Ilekes are washed in the solution and are now consecrated and have the Ashe. It is the Ashe that empowers the devotee with the essence of the Orisha." [34]

The Ilekes bring the protection of the Orishas to the individual. As with all aspects of Yoruba initiations there is a protocol, such is the same with receiving the Ilekes. One is expected to respect the Orishas and observe decent and moral behavior. The Ilekes are not to be worn while taking a bath, engaging in sexual intercourse or by women during their menstrual cycle. While this is the traditional view, Baba

Ifa has provided me with additional guidance concerning women during their menstrual cycles. He said to me via e-mail on May 18, 1998,

> "The Karade order does not prohibit sister-folk from any spiritual endeavor during her cycle, except for those ritual offerings that involve blood sacrifice. So, sisters may wear the Ilekes at those times when we know they are at their spiritual height. (The greater problem is their being educated to understand and channel the spiritual use of that cleansing phase)."

I realize the "traditional thinkers" may be up in arms regarding such a stand, however could it be that the Karade Order is seeking to correct an imbalance? Basically, the menstrual blood has been viewed with disdain. While this may seem an adolescent rationalization, what is menstrual blood if it is not sacrificial blood, the sacrifice of the unfertilized egg? Adding to this thought, Kisma K. Stepanich writes in her book, *Sister Moon Lodge, the Power and Mystery of Menstruation,*

> "The menstrual blood is the water of life, and should be held sacred. The word "sacred" often means taboo and vice versa. Like many ancient meanings that are twisted for the benefit of those in power, the meaning of taboo has been misconstrued, depreciated to negative connotations. Taboo, a Polynesian word which means: sacred, holy, menstrual, was generalized by anthropologists to mean "forbidden." It actually refers to what is empowered in a ritual sense as not to be touched or approached by any who are weaker than the power itself, lest they suffer negative consequences

from contact. The blood of women, menstrual or post-partum blood, is itself infused with the power that links women to the very heart of the universe. This power of woman is both heart (womb) and thought (creativity). Furthermore, the concept of woman power, or my power is related to the understanding of the relation-ships that occur between the waking dream (human life) and the dreamtime (nonhuman worlds)."

Women are seen as powerful beings, co-creators with God and are held in high esteem. It is during the menstrual years that a woman's power is the most potent, this explains why many Native American tribes did not want their braves sleeping with their wives during their moon time (cycle), the power was too much and needed to be set for the purpose of female transformation. Understanding this time of great power, Baba Ifa Karade encourages the Karade women to take part in ceremony (not to include sacrifices) and bring that power and insight into the community. At any rate, it will be the women who articulate their story in reference to the spiritual powers of the menstrual cycles. A much needed story indeed.

Additional instruction given to me concerning the Ilekes by Baba Ifa Karade was,

"In caring for your Ilekes, simply remember that they are sacred symbolic representations of the Orisha. You are to begin writing a 1 to 2 page report on each one of the Ilekes you now possess. When removing the Ilekes from your person, or when placing them on your person, attempt to face the east giving homage to Olodumare, the rising sun, Ile-Ife, our spiritual capital and Africa, our home. Hold the Ilekes up to the east as you make solemn prayer to the emanations. Touch them (as a group, not individually) to the third eye area and then place them around your neck.

If an Ileke breaks, gather all the beads that you can. Call me as soon as you can for further instruction. If someone touches them and you feel ill about it, wash your Ilekes in coconut milk and cool water. Let them sit on a white cloth until dry. Then you may begin to wear them again. You do not have to wear the Ilekes everywhere everyday. Be selective and protective of your new found treasure."

Before beginning the discussion on each Ileke that is presented to the new initiate, it should be noted that this section will involve a comparing of Yourba and Khametic concepts, along with Native American insights. Baba Ifa Karade constantly encourages us to look for the unity in this wonderful creation. Also, he and other scholars have presented research that, in part, the Yoruba nation migrated from a more distant eastern land. Lucas, in his work, *The Religion of the Yorubas*, points to the west african languages containing survivals of ancient khametic words. Ra Un Nefer Amen has shown the unity of our traditional cultures. It will be our attempt to point to this unity in our discussion of each Ileke, thus seeking to move the reader's consciousness from the Nile to the Niger.

Ra Un Nefer Amen demonstrates that a similarity exist between Yoruba and Egypt in his discussion of the concept of Deities. He points out that the names of the Yoruba Orisha, in essence are one and the same in terms of function and expression. Amen is Olodumare; Ausar is Obatala; Tehuti is Ifa/ Orunmila; Seker is Babalu-Aye; Maat is Aja Chagullia;

Herukhuti is Ogun; Heru is Shango/Jakuta; Het-Heru is Oshun; Sebek is Elegba;/Eshu; and Auset is Yemaya. Not only do the deities represent forces in nature, but different aspects of our spirit, and on fundamental level, our personality types.

In wearing the Ilekes, not only will one bring the protection of the Orisha to themselves, but they are reminded to display the qualities or characteristics of the Orisha.

The white Ileke is to Obatala. According to Baba Ifa,

> "Obatala is deemed the Arch-divinity of Yorubaland. Obatala represents the idea of ritual purity and ethical purity, symbolized by immaculate whiteness. Obatala is viewed as the most intelligent and even-tempered of the Orishas. Not only is he the "father of the Orisha," but also moulder of human form on Earth. He is the creative sculptor that forms the embryonic body of infants inside the womb. It was Obatala who first formed humankind out of the Earth's clay. Obatala is Olodumare's prime emissary on Earth."

Let's take a closer look at the notion of Obatala being Olodumare's prime emissary on Earth. In essence it means that Obatala represents, stands in for, or is Olodumare on Earth. Ra Un Nefer Amen in his momumental work, *Metu Neter Vol 1.*, points out that Obatala in Yoruba is the same as Ausar in Kamitic (Egyptian) philosophy. Besides being the Angelic emanations of the Creator manifesting through nature, Ra Un Nefer Amens shows that the Orishas, are the shaping factors of all physical structures, and events. The understanding of the functioning of these metaphysical vessels (Orishas, Neters, etc) is what constitutes the bases of African religion or way of life

If Olodumare/Amen represents the unmanifested aspect of the Creator, then Obatala/Ausar is the *first* manifestation of the Creator. Obatala/Ausar is the divine in-dwelling intelligence that guides all the functions of our spirit and the involuntary vital functions of our body. Obatala/Ausar is God dwelling in us as us!

In reference to Obatala/Ausar, Ra Un Nefer Amen states,

> "Perseverance in the identification with the in-dwelling intelligence in thought, speech, and action is the substance of *self knowledge*, which is essential for the individuals achievement of unity in his/her personal and social life, health and prosperity are achieved there by." [35]

Thus, it is the identification with Obatala/Ausar that will lead to a unified life here on Earth. Obatala is the owner of all heads, he is chief of all the Orishas. It is Obatala that they all pay homage to. Likewise, it is the Divine in-dwelling intelligence in us that all of our bodily and spiritual functions must submit to if we are to experience health and prosperity. There must be unity. Obatala/Ausar is the unifier. It is through Obatala/Ausar that we honor Olodumare/Amen.

The white Ileke represents Obatala/Ausar, it serves to remind us that God dwells in us and that the goal is to realize that state of divinity in this lifetime. It is said that Obatala is the father of the 401 Orishas and that he manages the affairs of man on earth. It is the divine in-dwelling intelligence that continues to keep our affairs in order. It is the divine in-dwelling intelligence that keeps all of our bodily, mental and spiritual functions in order without our conscious attention. It is as Baba Ifa Karade often says,

> "Everything is in divine order and Obatala represents that divine order."

If Obatala is representative of Olodumare on Earth, if Obatala/Ausar is the divine in-dwelling intelligence in man; then it would seem that in Native American Spirituality the eagle would represent Obatala/Ausar. According to Ted Andrews,

"Both the bald and the golden eagle have come to symbolize heroic nobility and divine spirit. These eagles are messengers from heaven and are the embodiment of the spirit of the sun." [36]

Eagles are messengers from heaven. Obatala is Olodumare's prime emissary on Earth. Emissary means an agent sent to represent or advance the interests of another. It is the eagle that brings the message of the Great Spirit; it is Obatala that represents the interest of Olodumare. Jamie Sams and David Carson point out in their book, *Medicine Cards*,

"Eagle medicine is the power of the Great Spirit, the connection to the Divine. It is the ability to live in the realm of spirit, and yet remain connected and balanced within the realm of Earth. The eagle soars, and is quick to observe expansiveness within the overall pattern of life. From the heights of the clouds, the eagle is close to the heavens where the Great Spirit dwells."

The white Ileke, Obatala/Ausar/Eagle reminds me of the unity of creation, the majesty of God and how blessed I am to have divine in-dwelling intelligence guiding my life. Thus one is reminded, as they wear the white Ileke of Obatala, that they are to seek, act and display wisdom in their actions. That purity of thought and morality leads to "Iwa-pele," one of the three stages that Orunmila provides for us in becoming a truly authentic human being.

The black and red Ileke is Eshu-Elegba. Eshu-Elegba is the keeper of the Ashe (essence of primal power and creative potential). He guards this power for the Orishas and humankind. Without it we could not make sacrifices or perform rituals.

In many respects it is Elegba who opens the way to higher laws and as a result of his guardianship of 'Ashe,' all sacrifices and offerings must be shared with him. Eshu-Elegba is the messenger divinity who delivers sacrifices to the Orisha from humans and from one Orisha to another.It is Eshu-Elegba who opens the way to other realities. Knowing both aspects of good and evil, Elegba is the negotiator between them. It is Elegba who brings us to the crossroad so that we may examine our living of the truth. Most times, when we find ourselves undergoing what we perceive to be a 'test'—trying to decide which action to take or which direction to proceed, it is Elegba who has brought us to this point. Are we going to give into that which is wrong or are we going to do that which is right? It makes no difference to Elegba which way you chose; Elegba will enforce the laws either way! He punishes as well as rewards. Therefore, Elegba is to be respected and honored.

In Khamit, Eshu-Elegba is known as Sebek and governs the intellectual faculty within our being. It also corresponds to the syllogistic logical mind which is highly dependent on information and governs communication. Ra Un Nefer Amen writes,

"Sebek is the faculty that enables us to separate and label parts of a whole, or members of a group on the basis of their external differences. Without this faculty we would look at an event, or thing and not be able to distinguish its parts or phases. Yet, because of it we segregate things, and events that belong together into air tight compartments, based on their superficial external differences, and thus create a host of problems in the world." [37]

Thus, we can see on one level why Elegba/Sebek is associated with mischief, chaos and confusion. It is this ability to segregate that we take as the ultimate reality, our being different. Instead of looking for the unity (Obatala/Ausar) in the multiplicity (Elegba/Sebek), we get caught in the multiplicity. Notice the next time Elegba/Sebek brings you to a crossroad situation. It is generally because you have failed to realize the unity and oneness of creation. You have strayed away from the directions of Obatala/Ausar! Conrad E Mauge, in his book, *The Yoruba Religion: Introduction to its Practice,*

> "As the Orisha who offers choices, he helps to control our day to day destiny. He is the one that presents situations to us each day that we must make decisions on. He sits at the crossroads and offers you several paths that you must choose from. He allows you to make the choice. Your decision; the action that you take, leads directly into your future. Elegba guards the door to the future and to future opportunity."

It is Elegba's/Sebek's ability to separate which allows him to show us the different roads we must chose from, when in reality it's all one road! Yet, the direction we travel must be based on divine truth, truth that is indicative of our level of consciousness and awareness. Let us look at an example: Elegba/Sebek brings you to the crossroads concerning a wallet you find laying on the ground and there is no one around to claim it, what do you do? One person's level of consciousness might be "finders keepers." Another's level of consciousness might be, knowing that God sees all, that the wallet is not theirs, therefore they would return it to its owner.

In both situations the person is acting on the truth based on their level of consciousness and Elegba will reward or punish accordingly. However, when a consciously evolved person acts in ways inconsistent with their level of consciousness, then, well you know what happens when your mother gets on you and says, "You know better!" The punishment is severe (smile). In essence, Elegba/Sebek causes us to get a good look at ourselves when we come to situations where we must decide between two directions. Elegba/Sebek is the opener of the way to greater understanding of self. Ra Un Nefer Amen writes,

> "Sebek corresponds to the side of Sebek as the guardian of the threshold. Sebek symbolized the crocodiles which closed the way to Arabians attempting to smuggle themselves into Kamit. We find the same throughout Africa where cognate deities like Elegba, etc. are also the guardians at the entrance of shrines, homes, etc. Anpu-called Anubis by the Greek and Apust (opener of the way), two aspects of the mercurial principle Sebek shared the duty of guiding the deceased in the underworld to Maat's Hall of Justice, where the heart (will) is weighed. The deceased in this case are symbols of the person undergoing spiritual initiation, as it results in dying to certain things in the world, as well as to the personality (see Seker)." [38]

Thus we see, that whenever Elegba/Sebek brings us to a crossroad where we might examine our living of the truth, it is a form of initiation. If we are serious about our spiritual growth and development, then when we come to a crossroad situation we must live truth. In living truth our false personality dies, our ability to hide behind rationalizations for wrong actions dies, we must live truth!

In Native American spirituality, the coyote is called the trickster. Coyote is the master trickster who tricks himself. The coyote is sacred, for in the folly of his acts, he can see his own foolishness. It is the acts of Elegba/Sebek/Coyote that allows us to see ourselves that we might become better people along this path.

Thus, the Ileke of Elegba reminds us that when they are at a cross road situation, it is Elegba who has them there, that they might examine their living of the truth. " Why am I in this situation?" "Is this justice coming back to me?" "Have I been disrespectful to the Orisha?" Yes, Elegba guards the cross roads and it is to Elegba that we give offerings to first, so that he might open the way to the other Orisha.

We want to be aware of the positive traits of Sebek/Elegba and seek to display them as they deal with the various cross situations in this life's journey. Those who have Elegba/Esu/Sebek as an incarnation objective must understand that they cannot take the information they have as knowledge. They must make sure that their information base reflects reality. Also, they must take time to understand what beliefs can do to you through the power of the mind. They must learn how to use the power of belief and how to avoid being victimized by holding on to wrong beliefs. Eshu-Elegba/Sebek is ruled by the planet Mercury, and thus these people are very quick witted and great communicators. Sometimes, however there is a tendency to communicate information and mistake it for knowledge. We see that lots of scientists have information but lack knowledge. They spend millions of dollars to put drugs on the market that kill people. They are informed but lack knowledge. So people with Eshu/Elegba/Sebek must be careful not to mistake information for knowledge. They must always be examining their belief systems, for our beliefs effect our behavior. If they only have information and that information does not reflect reality and they believe it to be true, then they will act on it. This explains why many of us can talk the talk, but not walk the walk.

Eshu-Elegba/Sebek people deal with details, they note the differences in things and are very analytical. In their relationships, communication plays a very important part. They must not put so much in the communication and the communication exchange, as to oppose the value of the message. Also, Sebek people can be critical and opinionated, so they must take these aspects into account when considering negotiations.

The yellow Ileke is Oshun. Oshun is the Goddess of beauty and love. It is said that she represents all of the feminine qualities. She is known for her free spirit, and her willingness to assist all who come to her for aid. Baba Ifa Karade writes:

"Oshun is the Orisha of unconditional love, receptivity and diplomacy. She is known for her sensuality, fine artistic development and beauty. Oshun is a river divinity symbolizing clarity and flowing motion. She has powers to heal with cool water and to divine based on her dream revelations and sensual perception. Oshun is said to have many sides. On the one hand, she can be very short-tempered and irritable. On the other, she can be calm and fluid. Either could be the case depending on the devotee and/or the nature of the situation. Oshun is also the divinity of fertility and feminine essence. Women appeal to her for child-bearing and for the alleviation of female disorders. She is fond of babies and is sought if a baby becomes ill. Oshun is reflected in brass, gold, and shining gems. She is known for her love of honey." [39]

In Khamit, Oshun is known as Het-Heru and she governs the faculty of imagination and creative visualization. It is through the faculty of imagination that we lay the foundation of what we want to accomplish. However, this foundation must not be made on what gives us pleasure. If this is the case then it will lead to addictions. Oshun/Het-Heru being that which is beautiful, sensual, and pleasurable can get so caught in these sensations that she can get lost. How many relationships end after the pleasure of sex deminishes? How many marriages end once the physical beauty changes?

We must take pleasure in our efforts to evolve to the level of Obatala/Ausar. For so many of us, spiritual cultivation lacks pleasure and joy. Oshun/Het-Heru is here telling us to enjoy the growth and development. Ra Un Nefer Amen writes,

> "The gonads are the organs represented by Het-Heru. Her name literally means, House (Het) of Heru (the libido, erotic force, sexual vitality that supports the will). The proper care of the gonads (prostate in the man, ovaries in the woman) and the judicious cultivation of pleasure builds up our libido (the power behind our will, ambition, psychic power, etc.). Unlike the Aryan religion, which in typical Sebekian fashion, segregate pleasure from the divine, Black religions have always understood that spiritual liberation depends on assigning the proper place to each thing in the world. The

quest for pleasure must not lead us. Pleasurable acts are to be allowed only after they have been investigated and found to be in conformity with truth, and always in due measure. Can you imagine the effect on a people's consciousness and spirituality if every time they engaged in sex, their attention was directed to the achievement of a spiritual God? What if they thought of themselves as engaging, not in a more carnal sense, but as divine beings using the energies of the lower part of their spirit to bring forth the higher?" [40]

Oshun/Het-Heru is here to bring us joy and pleasure. However, our quest for joy and pleasure must be in harmony with truth and in due measure. If Oshun\Het-Heru represents the female qualities, then in Native American spirituality she would be associated with the otter. Jamie Sams writes,

"The medicine held by otter is a set of lessons in female energy. Otter is the personification of femininity: long, sleek, and graceful, otter is the true coquette of the animal world. This joyful little creature is adventuresome and assumes that all other creatures are friendly-until proven otherwise. These character traits are the beauty of a balanced female side, the side of ourselves that creates a space for others to enter our lives without preconceptions or suspicions." [41]

As we seek to enjoy the growth of spiritual development, that joy should be shared with the whole community. Oshun/Het-Heru/Otter reminds us to go forth in the world and seek pleasure, in due measure based on truth, and always share that pleasure.

In many respects wearing the Ileke of Oshun reminds one that they are to bring sweetness into the lives of others as well as their own. That we as priest and priestesses must seek to restore harmony were there is none. That this should be done in a gracious manner. It is with a highly developed sense of intuition that will enable us to do the needed healing work of self, community and humanity. It is important for those of us who represent this spiritual path to always put forth the proper image and ensure that our society is evolving in the direction that the Egun and Orisha encourage.

People with Oshun/Het-Heru incarnation must pay attention to the images that go into their mind. They must also pay attention to the images that are associated with joy. They must be careful not to look outside of themselves for joy and that the joy they seek must be cultivated from within. They must seek to get in proper harmony with joy for this is critical to them. While we all seek joy, the joy that we seek must come from within. So many of us are looking outside ourselves for joy. We look for it in things, in people, and in situations. When not found, then turning to drugs and alcohol in an effort to anesthetize the pain and disappointment often becomes the path of least resistance. Is it any wonder that so many people with the most of things (wealth) are so unhappy, victims of broken marriages, and take more psycho drugs than any one! They are looking for joy outside of themselves. Have you ever noticed the joy a child has playing with simple things, they use their imagination and creativity to bring forth internal joy. Maybe we all should consider doing the same. Oshun/Het-Heru people are artist, romantics, and creators of beauty.

The blue Ileke is Yemoja: The Orisha Yemoja is our Mother. In fact she is said to be the Mother of all Orishas. While Obatala plants the seed, it is Yemoja that nurtures it to maturity. Yemoja rules over the womb; she is the amniotic fluid. It would also stand to reason that she rules over the earth, seeing how the earth is enveloped in an atmosphere of fluid. She rules us because the body is two-thirds water. Yes, Yemoja is our Mother, ruler of the rivers, the healing waters. She is caring, benevolent, accommodating, and dedicated.

In Kamit, she is known as Auset and is the embodiment of our intuitive and instinctive faculties that are deep within our psyche. In order to access these faculties, it is necessary for one to do trance work. Thus, Yemoja/Auset deals with our ability to go into trance and access higher spiritual realms. Again, it is said that Obatala plants the seed and Yemoja nurtures it. In Kamit Auset/Yemoja was the wife of Ausar/Obatala; she was dedicated to Ausar/Obatala. This is saying to us that we must be dedicated to realizing the God in self. We must be dedicated to our spiritual growth and work.

As we are blessed to come into the understanding of our Ancient spiritual systems, we see it requires work to grow spiritually. It requires dedication to this path. Thus, it is our Mother Yemoja, who in a loving and benevolent manner, teaches us dedication. She draws us to her breast and nurtures us as we seek to journey within (trance) in an effort to access the God within (Obatala/Ausar). It is our Mother Auset/Yemoja who will correct us when we are wrong and yet love us still.

In Native American Spirituality, Yemoja/Auset could be identified with the turtle. The turtle represents Mother Earth; it is the personification of Goddess energy, and the eternal Mother from which our lives evolve. As Jamie Sams points out,

"We are born of the womb of Earth, and to her soil our bodies will return. In honoring the Earth, we are asked by Turtle to be mindful of the cycle of give and take, to give back to the Mother as she has given to us." [42]

Adding to this Ted Andrews writes:

"In Nigeria, the turtle was a symbol of the female sex organs and sexuality. To the Native Americans, it was associated with the lunar cycle, menstruation, and the power of the female energies. The markings and sections on some turtles total thirteen. In the lunar calendar, there are either thirteen full moons or thirteen new moons alternating each year. Many believe this is where the association with the female energies originated. The turtle is the symbol of the primal Mother."[43]

The wearing of the Ileke of Yemoja can remind us that as we seek to return our people to tradition, there is a need to nurture them in the process. Just as mother is dedicated to her child, we as priests and priestesses of our Ancestral traditions must also have the same level of dedication. As we build spiritual communities, we must create environments where people feel secure and comfortable; that they know they are loved unconditionally and that we are here to assist them in their return to the ways of their Ancestors.

People with Yemoja/Auset as an incarnation objective must learn how to deal with trance. We understand that the key to developing the powers of astral projection, clairvoyance, clairaudience and psychic powers is Trance.

The red and white Ileke is Shango; Ra Un Nefer Amen writes,

"Heru in Kamit, and Shango (Jakuta) with the Yorubas

is the archetype of mature manhood, fatherhood, male leadership and kingship." [44]

There are many stories written of Shango, the Great King. Baba Ifa writes,

"Shango is the deified alafin (ruler) of medieval Oyo which is said to have hung himself because of his overindulgence. His elevation to the Orisha realm was brought about by his devout followers. They merged him with the deity of lightning and fierce retribution known as Jakuta. Shango's symbol is the double ax mounted on the head of the holy statues or dance wands (Oshe Shango). Shango is the Orisha of the drum and dance. He possesses the ability to transform base substance into that which is pure and valuable." [45]

This double ax of Shango reminds us that success and power have a double edge, and it should never be abused or misused. The same ax that brought you power is the same ax that can take it away!

Heru/Shango in Kamit represents our will. Simply put, the ability to make right decisions. All of our decisions should be based on truth. This being the case, then one can understand why it is said that Shango does not like liars. We must stand on truth no matter what. It is our ability to exercise free will which will either destroy or establish our kingdoms.

For a kingdom to be ever lasting, it must be built on truth. Our decisions should not be swayed by our emotions; our will must not be swayed by emotions. All must be swayed by divine truth. The symbol of Shango/Heru in Native American spirituality is the hawk. The hawk is a bird with keen eyesight and a bold heart. In the exercising of our free will, we must be able to see the overall view and have the courage to follow the truth. The hawk is a trainable bird of prey which is saying to us that we can train our will to combat those emotions that are destructive to us and others

The wearing of the Ileke of Shango reminds us to be proud of the traditions of our ancestors and who they were: to be very zealous in the re-establishing of the traditions of our ancestors and be ready and willing to protect and fight for this truth. Those who have Shango/Heru as an incarnation objective must not make the mistake of acting on their emotions. They must never act on their likes, dislikes, pleasures or pain. They cannot go through life acting on their emotions and sensualism. They have come to earth to develop the ability to express based on free will, a decision that is taken in freedom of emotional pressure. They must act on the right decision, a decision that is based on the divine guidance. While we all must do this, it is the make or break thing for Shango/Heru people. Recall, it was not until Heru consulted with Tehuti (Orunmila) that he was able to defeat Set. Shango/Heru people must learn to consult the oracle in their major decisions. The oracle speaks not from emotion or sensualism, it is the voice of the Creator. These people should learn to rely on the oracle for guidance in their lives. Shango/Heru deals with leadership, the correct use of will, and freedom of choice.

IV. DIVINATION

We all come into this life with a purpose. In his book, *The Healing Wisdom of Africa,* Malidoma Patrice Some' says,

"The Dagara believe that everyone is born with a purpose, and that this purpose must be known in order to ensure an integrated way of living. People ignorant of their purpose are like ships adrift in a hostile sea. They are circling around. As a result, tribal practices emphasize the discovery, before birth, of the business of the soul that has come into the world. A person's purpose is then embodied in their name, thus constituting an inseparable reminder of why the person walks with us here in this world." [46]

Many of us will spend a lifetime seeking to learn and understand this purpose. In this quest for understanding we will journey down different paths, some of which are unnecessary. Think of the many wasted lives that we see each day. Lives wasted on a search to define oneself based on a standard that is anti-nature.

We all come into this life attuned to a specific vibration, yet we find ourselves seeking to function to the vibration of another. Take for instance a radio band, it goes from 87–108 and each of the different radio stations have a set frequency. Some stations can be found at 96.3 and others at 102.1, we will never find station 96.3 at 102.1, it will always be found at 96.3 because that is its assigned frequency. Such is the same with us, we come into this life attuned to a certain frequency and as long a we function in accordance to our frequency we will be successful. However, it is not that easy. We are pulled each day to function at a different frequency. We are pulled by the allure of this material world. For example, many of us want fame and riches. Now, this is not to say that this is bad. It is only to say that in most cases we are seeking it at the frequency that is not our frequency. As a result, our life seems to be out of harmony with the divine forces of creation. We try and try, yet we make no progress towards the realization of our purpose for being here, and we make little progress towards the fame and riches we seek. It is divination that can assist us in understanding that we are not functioning in accord to our frequency.

In short, divination is the process of communicating both internally and externally with the divine forces of creation, and oracles are the tools that facilitate such communication. One may come into this life attuned to the frequency of 96.3 and as long at they stay attuned to that frequency then the divine forces of creation will bless him/her. It is when one strays from that frequency that things begin to go astray. It is via divination that one learns that they are way down at 102.1 frequency and that is why things are not going correctly. The divination will reveal the necessary steps to move the individual back to their frequency of 96.3 and thus success. Baba Karade writes,

> "It is through the process of divination that seekers come to know of themselves and the forces that are shaping their past, present, and future lives. Through the process of divination, seekers come to understand the need for alignment with their most heavenly of selves and how to overcome the opposing forces that disrupt their efforts." [47]

This turning of the divine dial generally takes the form of rituals, sacrifices, and prayer. It is through prayer that one petitions God to turn the divine dial back to his/her frequency. It is also through prayer that one comes to the realization and gains the conviction that the divinties will turn the dial back to his/her frequency. Ritual is the technology that allows the turning of the divine dial. Sacrifice carries with it the power to bring about change and transformation. Essentially, it is through divination that one can learn their purpose for being here, and how to stay in harmony with that purpose.

An example of this can be seen in how the Dagara view material and physical problems from a cultural view and the role of the diviner. Malidoma Some' writes in his text, *"The Healing Wisdom of Africa,*

"The indigenous understanding is that the material and physical problems that a person encounters are important only because they are an energetic message sent to this visible world. Therefore, people go to that unseen energetic place to try to.repair whatever damage or disturbances are being done there, knowing that if things are healed there, things will be healed here. Ritual is the principle tool used to approach that unseen world in a way that will rearrange the structure of the physical world and bring about material transformation." [48]

Divination is the means that tells us which door in the unseen world we should approach.

"A Therapeutic View of the Ifa Religious Tradition"

by
Oloye 'Baba' Ifa Karade
6ᵗʰ World Orisa Conference, Trinidad, August 1999

PART I
THE PROBLEM

In stating the problem, Baba Ifa Karade says,

"The sciences embedded within traditional religions that are set to identify and resolve the conflicts, traumas, and pains of both the individuals and the community, are often the first to come under attack and endure the brutal disintegration brought about by invading and oppressive cultures."

This statement speaks to the damaging effects of proselytizing between religions. As Baba Ifa states, the traditional religions are embedded with sciences that can resolve the conflicts, traumas, and pains of both the individual and the community. One such science of traditional religions that has fallen victim to proselytizing is rites-of-passage. A tremendous conflict that we see today is between our male youth and the question of manhood. So many of our male adolescents are searching desperately for manhood. As a result, they are sometimes unwittingly programmed to destroy themselves, their families, and their communities. In gist, they are often being misguided.

It is the traditional science of rites-of-passage that was vital to our definition of manhood. It was a science designed to take the initiate from a passive existence in the community to an active role. Yet, due to the invading and oppressive cultures, this science was not seen as valid and, therefore it was abandoned. However, the situation in our communities today calls for a revival of this science. In his book, *Ritual*, Malidoma Patrice Some writes,

> "The fading and disappearance of ritual in modern culture is, from the viewpoint of Dagara, expressed in several ways: the weakening of links with the spirit world, and general alienation of people from themselves and others. In a context like this, there are no elders to help anyone remember through initiation of his or her important place in the community. Those who seek to remember have an attraction towards violence. They live their life constantly upset or angry, and those responsible for them are at a loss as to what to do" [49]

Our young people are angry. They are looking for their important place in the community. Also, it is the breakdown in intergenerational communication that is contributing to the emergence of rebellious youth and the development of conflicting values in our society. We, the elders, must prepare the vehicles of initiation for them in the tradition of our ancestors. It is no longer a question whether or not we need rites-of-passage programs. The behavior of our youth demands it! Thus, we see the need for the revival of this science. However, it is time now to return to tradition. Baba Ifa speaks of how, by having our traditional foundations shattered, which includes the shattering of our mental, emotional, and physical stability, we are caused to run to the oppressive Euro-dominant society in an attempt to find self again. This can be seen in our infantile attempts to replicate rites-of-passage in the Euro-Christian tradition.

PART II
INSIGHTS

Baba Ifa points out the important role that religion plays in the overall stability of a people. He further demonstrates how Western influenced therapists justify treating Africans as non-human. It is clear that people's religion influences their world view, and our relation with the world and universe is determined by our, as Baba put it, "symbols, icons, and sacred beliefs." If another comes among us and invalidates these—our symbols, icons, and sacred beliefs—they essentially invalidate us and our reason for being. It has been, and continues to be, our acceptance of this invalidation by those alien to us that leads to our demise as a people. As Baba proclaims,

> "Western influenced therapists have statistically demonstrated that they have a lower regard for African

people as well as related Aboriginal nations. They see the traditional bodies, mores, values, and ethos as dysfunctional and, again, in need of shattering and replacing. The consequence of such is the reduction of the traditional person. He/she then becomes maladjusted, suicidal, self-destructive, addicted, and non-existent in respect to self-esteem . . .. It must be fully realized that therapeutic methodologies and religious doctrines are as two sides of a spinning coin."

Traditionally, in most indigenous cultures, therapeutic methodologies are contained in religious doctrines. Once you destroy or invalidate the religion, you destroy the therapeutic methodologies. Today, we wonder why our people are so maladjusted. I contend, that it might be because of our persistent adherence to a religious doctrine that is based on our inferiority.

PART III
SOLUTIONS

It is clear from Baba Ifa's speech that the solution lies in our returning to *our* traditions. It is time that we have the courage to reach for our way of life and live it! Baba states,

> "We, as a generation, are able to strengthen ourselves by studying and applying the ancient wisdom systems. Ifa, the foundation of West African religious and cultural thought, is such a system. It has been passed on to us by way of our ancestors."

Thus, if the therapeutic methodologies are contained within

our belief systems, then those methodologies that can eventually lead us back to a stable way of life are within Ifa.

"As we strive to reach the balanced and divine states, opposition and resistance from the internal and external realms will be encountered . . ... However, as the Odu reveals, it is through adherence to Ifa, worship of the Orisa, reverence of the ancestors, and serious commitment that these disruptive forces are placated and averted thereby lessening their destructive impact on our lives."

The people must return to tradition, Ashe!

Conclusion

Who are we? Who are the descendants of the slaves that were brought to this country? What is our destiny? And, who is our God? We all search for meaning in a world that seems to be devoid of meaning when it comes to people of African descent. Yet, this world can give us definitions of who we are and what we are and this world is so very quick to seek to invalidate our efforts to define ourselves. However, it is my understanding that God is God and there is no God but God no matter how you see it. It is my understanding that the same God that caused the great prophets to rise up in the past and lay the foundation for the great religious systems of old is the same God today! I say that to say, that God today can raise up great seers and sages who can give to the world a new vision of the future. God can raise up individuals today who can look into the religious systems of old and bring a new vision to them. I say to you that the same God that raised up our great prophets can raise them up today. I say to you that God can and will raise up among the African-American people great seers and sages who will bring to the world a new vision to the religions of old.

Do we not see places on this earth where the fresh waters of the rivers and streams meet the salt water of the oceans? Is there not life that can exist in both waters? Then such is the same with the so-called religious philosophies of the world. We have in America a people who were stripped of all knowledge of self, culture and kind. Once stripped, they were filled with an alien understanding of self. And, in time, these people evolved into something totally different than who they were originally. They evolved in the west, they became products of a western mentality, but encoded into their genes was a homing mechanism that would continue pushing them towards home and answers. In time they would find home, the religions of home—but how will they fit? Here, they were a people who for all practical purposes had a European mentality trying to understand an African reality! Such conflict: what a dilemma! Here, they are looking at Africa through white eyes and many were unable to truly understand what it is that they see. They would go to African religions and bring a European mind to the study of it. They would seek to completely transform themselves into Africans and cover up the Native American that runs through their veins and influence their world view. So what are they to do? Just as you have life that can exist in both the fresh water and salt water, you have a people who can combine both views and see very clearly. Today, it is time for these people—Africans born in America, filled with the blood of Native Americans to take the religions of home and seek to put them in a language that they can understand and truly relate to beyond being a fad!

This brings us back to our original question. Who is the God of Africans born in America? What religion do we have that is based on the geographical peculiarities of this American culture? What are the customs and philosophies which have been handed down to us by our Ancestors here in America? We must also bear in mind that when we reach for the religions from Africa, we are reaching with western hands and those religions must be brought into harmony with that understanding.

When we approach the concept of God in the Yoruba tradition we learn of the name, Olodumare. Olodumare is the Creator and we learn that all manifestations of creation are but different aspects of Olodumare. Olodumare stands behind creation and is unmanifested and unknowable in its entirety. When you look at the term *Olodumare*, it beaks down to:

<u>Olo or Ol = Owner</u>, <u>Odu = primal essence</u> and <u>Mare= go back to</u> *(the primal essence, in the beginning was the primal essence and the essence was God and the primal essence took on form).* So Olodumare means owner of the primal essence that I should go back to. "That one day I," as the Native Americans say, "will lay down my robe and return home to God in my true unconditioned state. That I would die a physical death and return to God." While we understand what this means in the metaphysical sense, it can also be applied to Africans born in America in respect to our quest. That we would have to lay down our western-conditioned mindset and return to African religion in an unconditional state.

It is time that we Africans born in America have faith that Olodumare (God) had a divine purpose for allowing us to come to this part of the world in the manner that we did. We are a new people, a different people, a people that know both worlds very well. Yes, I thank Olodumare for the guidance back home to the religion of my Ancestors. However, I realize that I must put it into a form that I can truly comprehend as a product of western society. I fully realize that I am but a young soul on this journey back home to the wisdom of my Ancestors and there is yet so much to learn. At this point I am certain of one thing, Olodumare did not have my Ancestors to suffer in vain. That many of us would come along and reach back across the sands of time and reclaim our lost heritage, combine it with who and what we are today, and give the world a new vision.

I say to the reader of these words, please understand that I, like yourself, am trying to make sense of our sojourn in America. I am looking deep into the psyche of our people trying to ascertain Olodurmare's purpose for it all. In my search, I do not profess to have all of the answers. I pray that as you read these words you will understand they are from a fellow seeker along this path of spiritual enlightenment, that I too am a brother seeking to return home to the ways of my ancestors.

The story is told that God called all of the warrior Kings and Queens together in Heaven. God said to them that the earth was going to fall under a time of being ruled by separation and fear. God said volunteers were needed to return; however they would have to be individuals of uncommon courage because they would be called to walk a way that was different from the rest of the people. That the people would think them crazy and weird, that they would seek to kill them (physically and spiritually). Yet God, Olodumare, assured them that all would be well. Dear reader, it is we who have volunteered to return!

Peace & Love,
Koleoso Oduneye Karade

NOTES

1. Mbiti, John S., *African Religion and Philosophy*, pg. 158

2. Some', Malidoma Patrice , *Of Water and the Spirit*, pg. 185

3. Karade, Baba Ifa, *The Handbook of Yoruba Concepts*, pg. 3

4. Clark, Walter Houston, *The Psychology of Religion*, pg. 232

5. Trungpa, Chogym, *Cutting through Spiritual Materialism*, pg. 20-21

6. Karade, Baba Ifa, *Imoye: A Definition of the Ifa Tradition*.

7. Wilson, Amos, *The Falsification of Afrikan Consciousness*, pg. 127

8. Ani, Marimba, *YURUGU*, pg. 168

9. Karade, Ibid

10. Wilson, Amos, Ibid pg 35

11. Karade, Baba Ifa, address at the "5th Orisha World Congress," San Fransico, Ca., 1997

12. Karade, Ibid., "5th Orisha World Congress."

13. Myers, James E. and Arthur C. Lehman, *Magic, Witchcraft and Religion*, pg. 104

14. Ra Un Nefer Amen, *Metu Neter Vol. 1*

15. Amen, Ibid, 128

16. Walsh, Roger N., *The Spirit of Shamanism*, pg. 38-39

17. Eliade, M., *Shamanism : Archaic Techniques of Ecstasy*

18. Miller, Patrck D., article in "Yoga Journal", July/August 1994, Issue 17, pg. 58

19. "Body, Mind, Spirit Magazine," January 1995, interview with Malidoma Some'

20. Matthews, Caitlin, "Singing the Soul Back Home, Shamanism in Daily Life."

21. Ring, Kenneth, *The Omega Project*, pg.214

22. Kalweit, Holger, *Dream time and Inner Space*

23. Ring, Kenneth, *Heading Towards Omega*, pg. 50

24. Kalweit, Ibid. pg. 6

25. Ring, Ibid. 215

26. Matthews, Ibid.

27. Myers, James E. and Arthur C. Lehman, *Magic, Witchcraft and Religion*, pg. 87

28. Myers, Ibid. pg. 86

29. Myers, Ibid. pg. 86

30. Lucas, J. Olumide, *The Religion of the Yorubas*, pg.179

31. Lucas, Ibid., pg. 179

32. Armah, Ayi Kwei, *The Healers*, pg.84

33. Karade, Baba Ifa, *The Handbook of Yoruba Religious Concepts*, pg.101

34. Karade, Ibid. pg. 100

35. Amen, Ra Un Nefer, *Metu Neter Vol. 1*

36. Andrews, Ted, *Animal Speaks*, pg. 139

37. Amen, Ra Un Nefer, *Metu Neter Vol. 1*

38. Amen, Ibid. pg.233

39. Karade, Baba Ifa, *The Handbook of Yoruba Religious Concepts*, pg. 26

40. Amen, Ra Un Nefer, *Metu Neter Vol. 1* pg. 150

41. Sams, Jamie, *Medicine Cards*, pg.64

42. Sams, Ibid., pg. 77

43. Andrews, Ted, *Animals Speaks*, pg. 364

44. Amen, Ra Un Nefer, *Metu Neter Vol. 1.*, g. 184

45. Karade, Baba Ifa, *The Handbook of Yoruba Religious Concepts*, pg. 27

46. Some. Malidoma Patrice, *The Healing Wisdom of Africa*, pg.3

47. Karade, Ibid , address at the "5th Orisha World Congress"

48. Some, *The Healing Wisdom of Africa*, pg. 23

49. Some, Malidoma, P., *Ritual*, pg. 30

BIBLIOGRAPHY

Abimbola, Wande. *Ifa and Exposition of Ifa Literary Corpus.* Athelia Henrietta Press, New York, 1977

Addae, Erriel Kofi, *To Heal A People*, Kujichagulia Press, Columbia, Md. 1996

Akbar, Na'im, *Visions for Black Men,* Mind Productions & Associates, Inc., Tallahassee, Fl. 1991

Akbar, Na'im, *Light from Ancient Africa,* Mind Productions & Associates, Inc, Tallahassee, Fl. 1994

Akbar, Na'im, *Know Thy Self,* Mind Productions & Associates, Inc, Tallahassee, Fl. 1998

Amen, Ra Un Nefer , *Metu Neter Vol. 1,* Khamit Corp. Publishing, Brooklyn, NY, 1990

Amen, Ra Un Nefer, *Metu Neter Vol. 2,* Khamit Corp. Publishing, Brooklyn, NY, 1994

Andrews, Ted, *Animal-Speaks,* Llewellyn Publications, St. Paul, Minnesota, 1997

Badejo, Diedre, *Osun Seegesi,* Africa World Press, Inc., Trenton, New Jersey, 1996

Bascom, William, *Sixteen Cowries,* Indiana University Press, Bloomington Press. 1980

Brown, Joseph Epes, *The Sacred Pipe,* Norman & London: University of Oklahoma Press. 1953

DeLubicz, Isha Schwaller, *Her-Bak:Egyptian Initiate,* Inner Traditions, Rochester, VI 1892

Ed McGaa, Eagle Man, *Mother Earth Spirituality,* Harper San Franciso, New York 1990

Eliade, Mircea, *Rites and Symbols of Initiation,* Spring publications, orginally published:

New York : Harper Bros. 1958

Epega, Afolabi A. & Neimark, Philip John, *The Sacred Ifa Oracle,* Athelia Henrietta Press, Brooklyn, NY 1995

Ephirim-Donkor, Anthony, *African Spirituality,* Africa World Press, Trenton, New Jersey 1997

Fatunmbi, Awo Fa'lokun, *Iwa-Pele, Ifa Quest,* Original Publications, Bronx, NY 1991

Fatunmbi, Awo Fa'lokun, *Awo:Ifa and the Theology of Orisha Divination,* Original Publications, Bronx, NY 1992

Fatunmbi, Awo Fa'lokun, *Iba 'Se Orisha,* Original Publications, Bronx, NY 1994

Idowu, E. Bolaji, *Olodumare, God in Yoruba Belief,* Original Publications, Plainview, New York 1995

Karade, Baba Ifa, *The Handbook of Yoruba Religious Concepts,* Samuel Weiser, York Beach, ME. 1994

Karade, Baba Ifa, *Ojise: Messenger of the Yoruba Tradition,* Samuel Weiser, York Beach, ME. 1996

Karade, Baba Ifa, *Imoye: A Definition of the Ifa Tradition,* Athelia-Henrietta Press, Brooklyn, NY 1999

Lucus, J. Olumide, *The Religion of the Yoruba,* Athelia Henrietta Press, Brooklyn, N.Y., 1996

Bibliography

Meadows, Kenneth, *Earth Medicine,* Elements, Rockport, Mass. 1989

Meadows, Kenneth, *Shamanic Experience,* Elements, Rockport, Mass. 1991

Mehl–Madrona, Lewis M.D., *Coyote Medicine,* Scribner , New York, NY. 1997

Oshoosi, Alashe Michael, *African Spirituality versus the African American*, Ibi' Koni Orisha, Inc., Berkeley, Ca. 1996

Ring, Kenneth, *Heading Towards Omega,* William Morrow & Co., Inc., New York 1984

Ring, Kenneth, *The Omega Project,* William Morrow & Co., New York 1992

Ring, Kenneth, *Lesson from the Light,* Insight Books, New York and London 1998

Sams, Jamie & Carson, David, *Medicine Cards,* Bear & Company, Santa Fe, New Mexico 1988

Some, Malidoma Patrice, *Ritual,* Swan/Raven & Co., Portland, Oregon 1993

Some, Malidoma Patrice, *Of Water and the Spirit,* G.P. Putnam's Sons, New York 1994

Some, Malidoma Patrice, *The Healing Wisdom of Africa,* Penguin Putnam Inc, New York 1998

Some, Sobonfu E., *The Spirit of Intimacy,* Berkeley Hills Books, Berkeley, Ca. 1997

GLOSSARY

Ebo: animal and plant sacrifices to one's ancestors or to the orisha

Efun: white chalk-like substance taken from the earth for religious consecration

Ewe: herbs and plants

Egun: ancestor

Khamit: Original name of Egypt

Kamit: different spelling of the original name of Egypt

Modupe: thank you

Omiero: herbal solution used for spiritual baths and consecration of religious objects

INDEX

For FREE catalog
Books about the Yoruba Religion
Ifa and Orisha Worship
Cassettes, CD's and Videos
contact:

Yoruba Book Center
610 New York Avenue
Brooklyn, New York 11203
Telephone (718)774-5800
Fax (718) 467-0099
email: yorubabookcenter@yahoo.com